MW00737153

Library of Congress Cataloging-in-Publication Data

Looking back, leading forward : the chief business officer through the years.
p. cm.
ISBN 978-1-56972-010-3
1. Universities and colleges—United States—Business management. 2.
Chief financial officers—United States. I. National Association of
College and University Business Officers.
LB2341.93.U6L66 2012
378.1'06--dc23
2012020124

Editor: Sandra R. Sabo, Freelancer Writer
Design and Layout: Zaki Ghul, Consultant

NC6013

CONTENTS

FOREWORD

NACUBO thanks all the contributors to this publication for sharing their valuable perspectives, personal stories, and outlooks on the future of the chief business officer (CBO) profession: Patricia (Patty) Charlton; Nim Chinniah; Mary M. Lai; Wendy B. Libby; James (Jay) E. Morley, Jr.; Joseph (Joe) P. Mullinix; and Benjamin (Ben) F. Quillian, Jr. Your careers, life experiences, various career paths, and points of view are an inspiration for us all. While each story is unique in its own right, it is surprising how these life experiences mirror those of so many others in this profession.

In addition, many thanks are owed to John D. Walda for tirelessly conducting the interviews and cleverly steering conversations back to the purpose of the publication. To my colleagues, Marta Pérez Drake, vice president for professional development, for her universal vantage point; Tadu Yimam, director of online learning, for managing the project and delivery; and Kaysha Johnston, production and design manager.

Much appreciation is also given to the NACUBO 50th Anniversary Committee for embracing the concept of this publication wholeheartedly and providing early content guidance as well as a very thorough evaluation and review of the individuals to be featured.

Members of the NACUBO 50th Anniversary Committee served an 18-month term and met quarterly to discuss all the activities for the celebration. Many thanks to the following:

Ruth Constantine, Smith College

Danny Flanigan, Spelman College

Roger Lowe, Wichita State University

Gaye Manning, Southern Arkansas University Tech

John Palmucci, Loyola University Maryland

Sally Roush, San Diego State University

From NACUBO, Altovise Davis, Monica Dillingham, Earla Jones, Juliet Mason, Maryann Terrana, and Dorothy Wagener.

And last—but definitely not least—Sandra R. Sabo, the editor who brilliantly weaved each interview into a story, giving life to words and creating a masterpiece for decades of future-generation CBOs—I thank you.

Bill Dillon
Executive Vice President
Chair, NACUBO 50th Anniversary Committee

INTRODUCTION: PAST, PRESENT, FUTURE

By John D. Walda

JOHN D. WALDA

John D. Walda is CEO and president of NACUBO. In addition to building a framework for higher education congressional relations, he has established strong ties with sister associations as chairman of the Washington Higher Education Secretariat (2009–2011) and director of the American Council on Education (2008–2011). Before joining NACUBO, Walda was partner in the Litigation Group of Bose McKinney & Evans and senior vice president – federal relations for Bose Treacy Associates, LLC.

Prior to moving to Washington, D.C., he was president of the Indiana University Board of Trustees for eight years; chairman of the Association of Governing Boards; chairman of the Board of Clarian Health Partners in Indianapolis, which owns and operates the Indiana University hospitals; and chairman of the Indiana Lottery Commission. Walda was elected a fellow in the American College of Trial Lawyers; is a trustee for several institutions, including Carroll College and Stetson University; and serves as director of the Indiana University Foundation and the Yellowstone Park Foundation.

PAST, PRESENT, FUTURE

Unique to institutions of higher education, the role of the college or university business officer is an old one. Early universities defined the role as "primarily responsible for administering university finances" and called them treasurers, stewards, receptors, and even proctors. Drastically different from today's evolving role, the CBO position has shifted from solitary administrator to collaborative leader, and it has grown in stature over the decades as areas of responsibility have increased.

In the 50 years since NACUBO's founding, several factors have propelled the CBO out of the back office and into the senior leadership circle, including increasing government oversight, skyrocketing energy costs, changing student demographics and enrollment, and decreasing levels of government funding. By 1987, when NACUBO celebrated its 25th anniversary, CBOs emphasized the need to become a "Renaissance man (or woman)," capable of handling whatever financial, business, and administrative responsibilities were placed on a CBO's institutional plate. As NACUBO now celebrates its 50th anniversary, their predictions have proved right on target.

Inside, you'll find a brief glimpse into the position of the CBO, how it has evolved, and where it's heading. While it would have been enjoyable to speak to each and every one of our members, we researched and searched for your colleagues from a variety of institution types, career paths, and roles that would hopefully resonate on a broad but individual level. The interviewees were asked to answer the same set of questions, and their answers—in their own words—were transcribed into the chapters you are about to read. When developing the questions that eventually "made the cut," it was critical that this monograph remain useful to you, your successors, and your colleagues. Three areas that resonated and came to be the points of focus were the following:

1. Career – How they started a career in higher education, what significant influences impacted their work, and how mentors were an important component to where they are today.

2. Role – When the role of CBO transitioned to the "inner circle" of the president's cabinet and how the CBO can engage the academic side of the house.

3. Future – What the position will look like in 50 years and how economic trends today will set the stage for the future.

You'll read how the GI Bill rapidly expanded the student population on campuses nationwide, prompting institutions to undertake ambitious construction projects and expand staff. Most notably, you'll find that the invisible line between administration and academia has softened in the intervening decades. Along the way, the visibility—and responsibilities—of senior financial officers has risen markedly.

Not surprising to some, you'll find that the role of the CBO changes on an almost daily basis. I recall hearing how one interviewee said that on one day, she might take on the role of a psychologist, talking with employees concerned about their jobs. But, on another day, she might take on the role of a public information officer, talking with the media, legislators, trustees, or business representatives.

Similarly, another interviewee's portfolio expanded to include more operational responsibilities, with both the chief information officer and the university's police chief now reporting to the CBO in addition to overseeing the facilities, human resources (HR), risk management and audit, environmental health and safety, financial services, business diversity, and real estate.

Likely, the most encouraging and profound discovery was the depth of professional encouragement and friendship these colleagues shared. Each interviewee could vividly recall colleagues at other institutions offering valuable advice on developing careers and solving problems. For instance, our regions have had a tremendous positive impact on the membership—not only did they create NACUBO, but on a personal level, they even precipitated the eventual marriage of one interviewee. They also provided venues for robust discussions and new discoveries, such as the (then) new IBM tabulating machine that could mechanize student registration and billing.

When NACUBO was founded in 1962 by the regional associations, it further impressed upon the profound impact networking had on the profession—especially with those at smaller schools, who could now reach out and discuss issues with colleagues outside their respective regions. It was almost with reverent voices that the interviewees described the absolute willingness to freely share information with colleagues that truly sets higher education apart from other fields.

Having had the pleasure of talking with all the authors personally, I appreciate the candor they demonstrated in these articles. I encouraged them to use this opportunity as a chance to share what was on their minds and in their hearts, and they took full advantage of that invitation. We are all the fortunate recipients of their insights and observations. Many lessons, valuable advice, and tips for success reside within these pages—not to mention some great stories.

SIGNS OF THE TIMES

By Mary M. Lai

MARY M. LAI

Mary M. Lai has been treasurer emerita and senior advisor at Long Island University (LIU) since retiring in 2003, after nearly 58 years as the university's CFO. She began her career as a public accountant with Arthur Young and Co., after completing her BS in accounting and economics at LIU. Lai, who resides in Brookville, New York, received her MS from Fordham University and was awarded honorary doctorates from LIU and Fordham University.

The numerous honors presented to Lai include NACUBO's Distinguished Business Officer Award, the Soroptimist Woman of Distinction Award, and the Model of Faith Award from Campus Ministry; she was also named Executive of the Year by the Institute of Management Accountants. LIU has bestowed on Lai the Woman of Achievement Award from LIU Post, the Metcalfe Outstanding Alumna Award, and the Outstanding Business Woman Award from the College of Management. She has served on the governing boards of numerous community service organizations, businesses, education associations, and professional organizations. Lai, a past president of both EACUBO and NACUBO, is a trustee at St. Joseph's College, a past trustee of Boston College and LeMoyne College, and a member of evaluation teams for two higher education accreditation associations.

SIGNS OF THE TIMES

As a little girl, I was always more interested in playing school than in playing house. So, after majoring in economics and accounting at Long Island University (LIU), I planned to teach business subjects.

When I graduated in 1942, however, there were no teaching jobs because of the war. With so many young men having been drafted, even before Pearl Harbor in December 1941, the field of public accounting had begun opening up to women. Fresh out of school, I became the first woman hired by a mid-sized firm that had always hired men with two years of experience.

Never having worked in public accounting, my experience didn't get me the job—but, evidently, my appearance did. The firm said it hired me because I looked wholesome—it wouldn't have to worry about my working and traveling with the men on the staff. I must have passed the test, because six months later the firm hired another woman.

After working for about 15 months, I got married and joined my husband, who was in the Naval Air Corps. While he was stationed at Lake City Naval Air Station in Lake City, Florida, I worked as the bookkeeper at the Bachelor Officer Quarters (BOQ)—I ran the whole operation, including food service and the liquor mess, which did business with chits rather than cash.

When I first arrived, I couldn't understand why the BOQ was losing money. I soon figured out there were no inventory controls; for example, whenever the bartenders asked for liquor, we'd just give it to them. I told the mess boys they had to give me 15 chits before I'd give them a bottle of liquor—and soon we were showing a profit.

My husband was discharged from the service early in 1946. We returned to New York, and I returned to work as a public accountant for Arthur Young and Co. One day, while traveling on the subway from one client to another, I ran into a former professor of mine. The professor mentioned our meeting to Dr. Metcalfe, the president of LIU, who called me that night and asked me to come back to the university as the business officer.

Not According to Plan

I learned the university had been without a business officer for nearly six months. The staff had managed to collect tuition and prepare the payrolls but had never accounted for these transactions nor maintained the general ledger. Furthermore, the university was still reorganizing after declaring bankruptcy in 1943. Many of its early benefactors had lost much of their fortunes in the crash of 1929—just two years after LIU opened—and the young school had not fully recovered from the loss of its support before enrollment plummeted during World War II.

Obviously, my alma mater needed help—and the sooner, the better. I reluctantly agreed to work for the university for one year, to put everything in good order, update systems and procedures, train the staff, and seek my replacement. Then, I planned to return to public accounting, get my certification as a Certified Public Accountant (CPA), and teach at a university. I did not believe that working for LIU would help me grow professionally. Yet, the one year I intended to work there has turned into more than 66 years. What happened to my plan?

First, our enrollment grew from 800 to 5,000 in 1946—half of whom were attending on the GI Bill. To accommodate the burgeoning demand for education among returning veterans, we rented space in local high schools to hold evening classes and hired many faculty, some of whom had served in the Armed Forces during the war. In just the first year, the administrative staff grew from three (president, registrar, and me) to 17 people. (Because our salaries weren't competitive, I usually hired older women who wanted to return to work or outstanding young high school graduates to whom we offered tuition remission.) This tremendous growth in enrollment and payroll all had to be handled manually. Registering and billing students, collecting and banking tuition payments, and calculating and typing paychecks for faculty (who were paid based on the number of classes they taught) all had to be done by hand. I worked such long hours that my mother used to ask, "Why don't you bring a cot to work and just sleep there?"

In fact, I personally prepared all payrolls for faculty, who received monthly checks, and staff members, who were paid weekly in cash. Every Monday night, I would take home the staff payroll and calculate the cash denominations we needed to get from the bank. Then, the next day, we'd put the correct amount of cash in each envelope for the employees to pick up. At the time, students paid a flat rate of $150 per semester, or $300 per year, to attend the university. That tuition represented the entire operating budget; we did very little fund-raising and didn't receive any research dollars.

By the end of the first year, I had put so much of myself into the university that I didn't want to leave. Meanwhile, my husband had earned a master's degree from Columbia and had finished most of the course work for his doctorate. Our plan was to relocate outside of New York—until President Metcalfe offered him a position at LIU as assistant professor in health and physical education and assistant director of athletics (not to mention assistant basketball coach and baseball coach). My husband's acceptance of the offer was all I needed to continue in a role I had come to love.

Growth in Responsibilities

In 2003, when I was 82 years old, I gave up the CBO position to become senior advisor and treasurer emerita. Fifty years earlier, I had come close to leaving the university when I became pregnant; in those days, women with children simply didn't work. But, I didn't want to give it all up, especially when I realized there wasn't a procedure or piece of paper that I hadn't designed myself. Fortunately, a friend of my mother's was looking for a job, and she proved to be a great child-care provider. For me, someone who thought she never could have children—or keep working if she did, the way it all worked out emphasized that God wanted me to continue working at the university. (I used to pray, "If it is wrong for me to continue working, put obstacles in my path; if it is right, remove them.")

Certainly, my role changed through the years, reflecting the evolution of the business office within higher education. When first hired, for example, I had the title of bursar and spent most of my time training staff and creating systems to process large volumes of work. The bursar was the chief financial person at most schools; only large schools like Rutgers, New York University (NYU), and Columbia had a business manager in place over the bursar. The bigger schools usually hired men as their business managers, while many smaller schools had female bursars and registrars.

In the 1950s, things became more complicated as enrollments continued to grow and placed a greater strain on facilities. Most schools began hiring either a director of finance or a controller—usually someone who had been in the accounting field (always a male)—to whom the bursar then reported. When the federal government got into the act, colleges and universities added vice presidents to oversee programs authorized by the Higher Education Facilities Acts of 1963 and the Higher Education Act of 1965. In rare cases, like mine, internal candidates were promoted to this new layer of staff. And, it seemed to me that most of the time, the new vice presidents came from outside higher education, often from the military.

Another pivotal moment for business officers came in the mid-1970s. The U.S. economy was struggling, enrollment was declining after a period of tremendous growth, and the federal government had begun pulling back on the research it had been funding. During the building boom of the 1960s, many schools had overextended themselves, and the problems of the 1970s led to major budget issues. In response, some schools became more selective, and others changed their mission—for example, single-sex schools went coed.

As schools cut back on their budgets, more students and faculty wanted to get involved in the budget process to protect their areas of interest. At the same time, faculty and staff within higher education started to unionize. It was then that schools began setting up budget advisory committees and inviting faculty and students to attend board meetings; some schools even gave these groups seats on the board.

During this time, I remember Joe Whiteside, the treasurer of NYU, saying to me, "Isn't it great to have everyone listening to you for a change?" And, it was a change to have people looking to the CBO to identify solutions to the various financial problems. As the CBO, I didn't simply record financial activities anymore; I usually led the budget discussions. This usually meant making sure everyone on the committee understood what each part of the budget represented—and that if one part increased, then another needed to decrease to maintain stability.

At Long Island University, for example, our enrollment declined from 11,000 in 1968 to 3,000 in the 1970s at our Brooklyn Campus because of City University's new open enrollment policy. Fortunately, the rest of the university maintained its enrollment. Because we had excess faculty, I designed an early retirement program and instituted income and instructional cost analysis so we could determine faculty productivity.

Technology's Touch

Improved technology increasingly made financial information easier to come by. In the 1950s, our big step forward was installing a few NCR machines to help manage budgeting, accounting, payroll, and student accounts. In 1960, we put in our first mechanized registration and billing system—an IBM tabulating machine that used punch cards to produce a customized bill for each student. I had convinced the president that we should buy the machine rather than hire an assistant registrar, because the cost was about the same.

In the 1970s, working with financial and student services officers, my office developed an in-house, integrated system to handle student records, registration, course schedules, student accounts, accounting, payroll, budget, and general ledger. We continued to upgrade that until we made the decision to purchase an Enterprise Resource Planning (ERP) integrated information management system.

I remember hearing about that first IBM machine during an Eastern Association of College and University Business Officers (EACUBO) meeting. Through that group, I got to know the sisters from the Catholic colleges. Although some had been bookkeeping teachers, many of them needed advice on how to handle things at the college level, and I was delighted to help. It was harder for the sisters to talk to the men because they tended to be very reserved, banker types—and, back then, a woman didn't speak to anybody to whom she hadn't been introduced.

Eventually, some of us started talking about the need for a national association. I belonged to the National Association of Education Buyers (NAEB), the purchasing association, and the College and University Personnel Association (CUPA), the personnel association, both of which had a national organization, so why not one for business officers? Another catalyst was that in the late 1950s and early 1960s, the federal government was getting into everything within higher education. NACUBO's founding in 1962 helped us all, especially the smaller schools, to make national contacts and to talk to people outside our own region.

Where We're Headed

Just as U.S. economic and demographic changes influenced the CBO's role in the past, they will continue to do so in the future. What trends in enrollments, endowments, student services, government compliance, technology, and employee benefits—to name just a few areas—will continue? How should we reallocate resources? What new areas should we be studying? To help answer those types of questions, the CBO needs to provide relevant data as well as leadership to keep the university moving in new directions.

By remaining aware of changes in the external world that will affect enrollment and finances, the CBO can encourage the president's cabinet to anticipate responses to evolving circumstances. Looking ahead, these changes are likely to include the following:

1. Although a university's functions—and, therefore, its structure—will not change too much, some areas (such as HR) will grow more complex. Each vice president, for example, will need to become more conversant with how technological advances affect his or her area.

2. Planning will increasingly become tied to institutional effectiveness and accreditation. The vice president of planning position, however, may be eliminated because all vice presidents and the president must engage in institutional planning; the administrative functions associated with planning would continue but at a different level.

3. Collection of tuition and loan repayments will continue to pose problems even when the economy improves because tuition will continue to increase. At every meeting, the CBO must inform the board of the current year's budget, enrollment trends, and fund-raising results.

4. Faculty at more public institutions will unionize. In general, faculty unions will hinder higher education's ability to respond to change. To help faculty understand the financial implications of unpopular decisions—and why the decisions are essential to maintaining financial health—the CBO should work with the chief academic officer to develop income/cost analyses of existing programs and business plans for new enterprises.

5 The involvement of members of governing boards will grow. Increasingly, they will ask for more information and won't very easily accept what the administration says.

6. The future will put even more pressure on a president to excel in many areas—as a successful fund-raiser, an effective liaison to faculty, a team leader of all the vice presidents, and an overall leader who ensures morale remains high at all levels of the college or university.

More Than a Job

Having worked for nine presidents, I can truly say each one was different. One, a former admiral, seemed to resent the fact that I was a woman because he felt he couldn't cuss in front of me (and he liked to cuss). Another was brilliant but insecure, so he often put people down. One did not believe in decentralization or giving the vice presidents any authority to make changes. But, I got along with all of them by adapting my management style to gain their trust and support. I showed each one that I was a member of the team and would work hard to move the university forward.

The part of my job I loved the best was helping staff and students who had financial problems. We have a program that enables our staff to borrow money from the university, with the loan payments handled through payroll deductions. A lot of business officers may not like that, but we found it good for staff morale. I often met with students, who didn't pay their bills, to work out a payment plan, and some students still come to me for help with budgeting and saving money so they can continue their education.

For me, the decades as a CBO went by quickly because I was passionate about the university and cherished its mission of access and excellence. I loved the culture of the university, the collegiality, the team spirit; we were all committed to helping our students realize their goals.

I'm proud to report that today LIU offers more than 550 degree and certificate programs and educates more than 24,000 students at six campuses. Our current president has served as chief executive officer (CEO) since 1985. We are a proud, diverse institution, having served generations of students, many of whom are the first in their families to attend college. There are more than 182,000 living alumni. Our operating revenues are in excess of $400 million, and the endowment was valued at approximately $80 million as of February 2012.

Life—and Long Island University—have taught me that if every fiber of your being wants to succeed, no matter what you're trying to accomplish, then all your hard work is for more than just a job. When you love what you're doing, you'll love going to work every day.

EDUCATION FROM ALL ANGLES

By Benjamin F. Quillian, Jr.

BENJAMIN F. QUILLIAN, JR.

Benjamin "Ben" F. Quillian, Jr., is executive vice chancellor for business and finance and CFO for the California State University (CSU) system. In addition to developing and monitoring an annual budget of approximately $6 billion, he oversees financial reporting, risk management, public safety, capital planning and construction, and IT initiatives for the 23-campus system.

Before joining the office of the CSU chancellor in 2008, Quillian spent five years as senior vice president for business and operations at the American Council on Education. His prior experience includes serving as vice president for administration and CFO at CSU Fresno and as a tenured faculty member and administrator at Southern Illinois University at Edwardsville, where he ultimately became vice president for administration. Quillian holds a BA in elementary education from Harris Teachers College, an MS in education administration from Southern Illinois University, and a PhD in social relations in education from Washington University in St. Louis.

EDUCATION FROM ALL ANGLES

In the mid-1960s, I taught 7th and 8th grades at an elementary school in St. Louis. One boy—who was a C-plus, maybe B-minus, student—had a certain sparkle that convinced me he was much brighter than he ever demonstrated at school. So, when the opportunity arose, I nominated him to attend a private, college-prep high school.

Years later, I reconnected with that student from my inner-city classroom. As it turned out, he had graduated from that boarding school near the top of his class and earned a bachelor's degree in accounting—because, he says, I had once told him he was good at arithmetic. Then, he went to law school, became a CPA, and started his own financial services business. On the wall of his office hangs a framed newspaper story that quotes him as saying, "I owe all of this to my 7th and 8th grade teacher, Mr. Quillian." Talk about a badge of pride! That certainly made me feel as if I have had some success in my career as an educator and administrator.

Entry into Higher Education

After three years of teaching in that elementary school—making about $5,300 a year—I ventured into higher education for the first time. It was 1967, and Southern Illinois University at Edwardsville (SIUE) wanted to increase the diversity of its student body. My job, as a precollege counselor in the admissions office, was to visit inner-city schools throughout Illinois and recruit African-American students. The idea of helping young people get into the university setting was exciting to me (and the $8,000 salary was nice, too).

While at SIUE, I earned a master's degree in educational administration. There was a consortium of universities in the area, and I was asked to speak at Washington University in St. Louis about increasing the number of African=American students. Afterward, as I was getting ready to leave, the director of admissions at Washington University asked if I was willing to come and work there.

"No," I responded, "I'm not interested."

"Young man," he said, "when somebody asks you that question, at least get the details."

So, I asked for the details—and soon went to work in my hometown, as assistant director of admissions and financial aid at Washington University. While there, I became intrigued with higher education administration. Deciding that the only way to really go far in that direction would be to get a PhD, I left the workforce to attend graduate school full time. At the time, I had my choice of law school or graduate school because I had been admitted to both at Washington University. Deciding I would be happier in a position that was closer to helping young people, I pursued a joint degree of psychology and education, called social relations in education.

When I entered graduate school, I had my eyes set on administrative work. As I became immersed in the doctoral program, however, a radical change took place; I decided to become a faculty member. In fact, after completing the proposal for my dissertation, I returned to SIUE and joined the faculty as an assistant professor, eventually gaining tenure as an associate professor.

Students actually played a role in my leaving the classroom for administration. One of the graduate courses I taught focused on the rights of children and touched on the causes of juvenile delinquency—the topic of my dissertation. Some of my graduate students had learned the university was recruiting for its first affirmative action officer, and they encouraged me to apply for a position that matched my interests in the rights of children. I was fortunate to be chosen for the position—my first at what could be called the senior administrative level.

Multiple Mentors

Within a few years, I began reporting to a new president who became one of my mentors: Earl Lazerson. Earl spent his entire career at SIUE, moving from lecturer to professor, to chair of the math department, to provost, and to the presidency. From him, I learned how to get things done—even though I wouldn't necessarily do things in the same way he did. For example, Earl really used the power and authority of his position; he made sure the right people knew what he wanted and then gave the directive to get the job done. My approach tends to be softer; I usually use persuasion to get people on board with me.

Based on Earl's suggestion, I applied for Harvard University's Institute for Educational Management. Once there, I realized very quickly that I knew absolutely nothing about the business side of the university, so I focused on learning those aspects during my time at Harvard. When I returned to SIUE, Earl named me assistant vice president for administration, where I had personnel and a fair amount of budget responsibilities.

In 1984, again based on Earl's suggestion, I applied for a fellowship with the American Council of Education (ACE). During my time as an ACE Fellow in academic administration, I realized that I didn't want to be a university president—but I did want to be an administrative vice president and a chief financial officer (CFO). As part of the fellowship, I worked for a year with someone who became another mentor to me: John Biggs at Washington University.

Like me—but unlike most of the people I had encountered on the business side—John didn't have a business degree. He assured me that my level of financial understanding was more important than a degree. John gave me the courage and confidence to manage financial people by knowing how to ask the right questions (and how to detect when they're doing a snow job).

Not long after I returned to SIUE, I was promoted to vice president for administration. The university was still fairly young, so my position had less to do with money and more to do with physical planning. Although I had responsibility for payroll, police, and information technology (IT)—called "data processing" then, my focus was mostly on facilities and building the campus.

One day, I received a letter from John Welty, president of California State University (CSU) Fresno, encouraging me to apply for the position of vice president for administration and CFO. I'd been at SIUE for 15 years and had no thought of leaving, but Earl Lazerson encouraged me to investigate the opportunity. "I'd hate to lose you," he said, "but I think it would be a great next step for you."

Fresno turned out to be about 110 degrees and dusty—not exactly what a city guy like me wanted. But, I eventually accepted the position there, which was one of the best things I could have ever done. As a president, John Welty gave me the freedom to grow and be creative and the latitude to venture into various areas of the institution.

For example, I once served as interim athletic director for nine months, even though I didn't know anything about athletic administration. John assured me, "You're a manager. You can do this." Part of my job entailed mentoring some African-American athletes who were "misbehaving" (that's the polite way of putting it). The other part was reconnecting an athletic department acrimoniously split in two because of Title IX. Some were in favor of gender equity, while others were diametrically opposed. Coming in as an outsider, I could be more objective.

Being at Fresno took me into other areas of campus administration that I hadn't had experience in. During my time there, the campus built a large, multipurpose arena that required the selling of bonds, delicate negotiations with the city (which didn't want a new facility taking business away from its own arena), and liaison with the entertainment industry to promote the new venue. That one project exposed me to so much on the business side, from market analysis to events marketing and from capital financing to fund-raising.

A Desire for Change

After 10 years at Fresno, I received a call from Bill Hartley, who had been an ACE Fellow with me. He said, "There's a position at the American Council on Education that's perfect for you—senior vice president and CFO." I wasn't sure I, or my wife, was willing to leave California for Washington, D.C., but I flew out for an interview and really liked the place. So, for the next six years, I joined the world of higher education associations.

Being away from higher education institutions gave me an opportunity to see their flaws and inefficiencies more clearly. I gained insight into why many people were greatly concerned with how higher education operated. At ACE, I could talk candidly about the transformational changes that higher education needed to make, on both the administrative and academic sides, without worrying about what faculty members might think.

Although we talked and wrote a lot about transformation, ACE is primarily an advocacy and policy organization. The nitty-gritty of making change has to happen at the institutions themselves. As a result, when I returned to the CSU system in 2008, I brought a fairly high level of impatience about wanting to create greater efficiencies and really change how we do things.

Unlike many elite private institutions or some public research institutions, the CSU system can't call upon an endowment or research overhead to help us out. About 50 percent of our revenue is tuition, and we depend on the state for the other 50 percent. But, in recent years, the state has been less able or willing to fund us, which has repercussions all throughout the organization.

In FY2011 alone, we went through a $750 million budget reduction for our 23 campuses, with more cuts likely in the future. In large measure, that will mean dismantling what we normally do. We can no longer use one-time funds to essentially put a bandage on the budget to avoid major layoffs, avoid discontinuations of major programs, and avoid major enrollment reductions. Now, budget reductions must be sustainable for the long haul.

Unfortunately, for example, we may have to give out layoff notices. We know doing that will affect morale and prompt some of our talent to leave. At the administrative level, I am pushing for cost reductions through more collaboration among our campuses. Right now, we have 23 admission offices, 23 accounting offices, 23 of everything. But, it's much too costly for all 23 campuses to continue operating so independently. Although I'm not advocating a centralized model, I would like to see a shared service center approach, where select activities are moved to campuses that have strengths in those areas. And, we're looking hard at reducing the cost of utilities—for example, by using technology, such as photovoltaics (solar panels).

Most of the budget cuts have affected the administrative side. Still, the academic side needs to look at its organization as well: Does it need as many schools as it has? Does it need as many programs as it has? Which programs are overly expensive and under-enrolled? These are some of the tough questions the academic officers and faculty should address. They must identify their true needs and determine whether they are truly operating within their mission. And, maybe, they need to look at the mission statement itself and make some changes.

The need to provide value to our students really hit home for me the day I went to a local grocery store. The young woman who helped me mentioned that she had a degree in sociology from CSU. And, there she was, probably making minimum wage. Obviously, the college degree didn't have much value for her—and that conclusion, to me, really points to the need for us to innovate.

Future Focus

Perhaps because I come from the faculty and have spent a lot of time in classrooms during my career, I believe the CBO of the future must work more collaboratively with the academic side of the house. You can't just look at the books—which technically trained finance people tend to do. Instead, you have to be in tune with what the university is doing and why. That knowledge and understanding come only through frequent interactions and good relationships with the academic side.

Sometimes, taking that overarching look at the institution will lead to decisions that may not be ideal from a business sense. But, those decisions—provided they're not detrimental to the institution—should be made if they will produce outcomes that will benefit society, in general, and the students you serve, in particular.

A PRESIDENTIAL TRAINING GROUND

By Wendy B. Libby

WENDY B. LIBBY

Wendy B. Libby became the ninth president of Stetson University in 2009. Under her leadership, the university has experienced growth in student recruitment and retention; made major improvements to campus infrastructure; and expanded athletics to include three new Division I sports, including the return of football. From 2003 to 2009, Libby was president of Stephens College, where she led a successful strategic initiative to restructure academic programs, increase enrollment, and achieve financial stability.

Her other positions within higher education include serving eight years as vice president for business affairs and CFO at Furman University and as CFO at Westbrook College (now part of the University of New England). Libby, who earned both her BS (biology) and MBA (finance) from Cornell University, also holds a PhD in educational administration from the University of Connecticut. She currently serves on the board of directors for Mainstreet Community Bank in DeLand, Florida; is a past board member of EACUBO and the Council of Independent Colleges; and was a founding board member of the Private College 529 Plan (Tuition Plan Consortium).

A PRESIDENTIAL TRAINING GROUND

As an undergraduate at Cornell University in Ithaca, New York, the prospect of living the rest of my life in Ithaca, New York, seemed awfully delicious. Maybe that's why I stayed at Cornell for my master's, after completing my bachelor's degree in biology. Having no interest in medicine, I thought I would combine biology with business and have a career in hospital administration.

Although I completed Cornell's Sloan Program in Hospital Administration, I decided to earn my MBA in finance and work in private industry. After four years, however, the travel associated with the job took its toll—being out of town constantly was too hard on me.

The Sum of the Parts

When you live in Ithaca, it's logical to look for work at one of the universities. In 1979, I became director of administration for the public management program at Cornell's business school, which entailed handling admissions and helping students prepare resumes and find jobs. While I loved being in higher education—because it's mission driven, it's fun, and it's complex—I soon realized that my strengths did not lie in that type of work.

With the encouragement of several friends, I applied—and was hired—to be the director of administrative operations for Cornell University's College of Architecture, Art and Planning. That was my "side-door" entry into being a business officer, because I didn't have the classic background of having been an accountant. Jack Ostrom—Cornell's controller, a longtime NACUBO member, and winner of the Distinguished Business Officer Award—believed that anyone who was the business officer of a unit should have the opportunity to move up the ladder at Cornell by understanding how the whole university worked. He ran a summer program for us that provided the theoretical underpinning for why universities do what they do financially, enabling us to understand not only the industry but also the impact on Cornell, in particular.

I learned, for example, why the College of Architecture, Art and Planning got hit with a heavy dose of overhead every year—and why the college's low faculty-to-student ratio meant there was nothing I could ever do to break even. To this day, I still have the notes I took during that summer program.

At a Western Association of College and University Business Officers (WACUBO) business management program, I met my husband Richard. When he accepted a position as executive director of the State Technical College System of Connecticut, I became assistant director of the University of Connecticut's John Dempsey Hospital. The two years in that position reinforced my resolve to never work in health care again, so in 1987, I moved to the University of Hartford as the senior HR officer and special assistant to the president.

Two years later, Westbrook College in Portland, Maine, hired me as its CFO. At the time, Westbrook—which is now part of the University of New England—was in really tough shape. In fact, on one of my first days on the job, I had to go to the bank and ask for help in working through the college's financial crisis. In the six years I spent at Westbrook, we had many difficult conversations, not unlike the ones many colleges are probably having today with their boards of trustees. For Westbrook, the central issue was that it had been a two-year women's college that waited probably 15 years too long to become a coed, four-year institution.

The benefit of working at an institution having financial difficulties is that you learn about all the different functions, about everything that makes a college or university whole. By 1995, in addition to gaining this on-the-job experience, I had finished my doctorate at the University of Connecticut in educational administration and was ready for a new challenge. (Incidentally, my dissertation looked at organizational behavior differences at land-grant institutions in states with and without a high level of regulation. I hardly thought it a groundbreaking topic yet; years later, the impact of state regulations on a public university's organizational climate and operating results has become quite important.)

Aiming for the Top

My next move was to South Carolina in 1995, where I became vice president for business affairs and CFO at Furman University. A few years earlier, the university had cut its formal ties with the South Carolina Baptist Convention, its chartering organization. David Shi, the president guiding Furman's emergence as a fully independent university, had vision and energy—and the support of a committed group of alumni and board members who understood the ownership of the institution was now in their hands.

For me, going from Westbrook to Furman was like moving from poverty to riches overnight; Furman did not have one dollar of debt on its books. It also had several million dollars in what, back then, we called the unexpended plant fund, plus quality academics and an effective fund-raising apparatus during an upswing in the stock market —all the ingredients needed to fund and dramatically enhance what was already a beautiful campus. We not only had the means to grow the university but also could be daring in how we did it. This burst of energy, which emphasized that Furman was an institution on the move, led to 28 capital projects in the eight years I worked there.

I could have remained at Furman and been very comfortable. Or, I could have moved to a more complex private institution or to public higher education as a CFO. Instead, with my husband's encouragement, I decided to pursue a college presidency.

After expressing interest in four or five vacancies but never getting an interview, I contacted Barbara Taylor, an academic executive search consultant. Her firm, steady voice told me that my cover letters didn't communicate that I cared about the position itself—I just stated the facts and enclosed my resume. Barbara recommended customizing each cover letter to the particular position. If, for example, the advertisement listed eight qualities a school wanted in its new president, I needed to explain how my experience related to each of those points. As soon as I changed my cover letters, I started getting interviews.

I contacted Barbara again when I received an offer from Stephens College in Columbia, Missouri. Again, her advice proved invaluable when I expressed concern about the college's financial condition and long-term ability to survive. She said, "Look, you don't have to make this your life's decision. If you spend a few years there, making the college viable, you can always move somewhere else." I had never thought of serving as president of Stephens College as an intermediate step—but, as it turned out, that's exactly what it was.

Survival Tactics

When I became president of Stephens College in 2003, the private, four-year institution was in frail financial health. Enrollment was down, the college had been operating for years with a deficit, and it didn't have an endowment that could support competitive financial aid packages. Nor did Stephens have the amenities offered by many of its competitors, in either the women's college or small coed college markets. In fact, I believe the search committee selected me—someone who had not followed the normal route to a college presidency—because I understood the financial side of higher education.

The biggest question was whether Stephens should remain an all-women's undergraduate institution. Looking at the academic mix—which included a fashion design program and a theater and dance program, each of which represented one-third of our enrollment—it became clear we needed to remain a women's college. But, to survive, we needed to sharpen our focus and concentrate on strengthening the unique programs Stephens offered. The college, for example, had long been known for its program in equestrian studies, yet enrollment in that program had dwindled to about 12 majors.

Through a five-year strategic initiative dubbed The Renaissance Plan, we built the equestrian program back up to 80 majors (and 60 horses) and reinvigorated other academic areas as well—for example, by introducing new majors in theatrical costume design and digital filmmaking and starting "plus-one" programs for earning a master's degree. Part of the renaissance entailed reclaiming pieces of our past, which included renovating several historic residence halls, offering summer courses (for the first time in nearly a decade), and reestablishing partnerships with local community organizations and other educational institutions. We also moved from National Collegiate Athletic Association (NCAA) Division III to the National Association of Intercollegiate Athletics (NAIA) to attract students and allow us to offer athletic financial aid.

Within five years, we had reduced operating deficits to the break-even point, established an endowment foundation, and embarked on a successful comprehensive campaign. Full-time undergraduate enrollment increased 72 percent, and enrollment in graduate and continuing studies programs increased 150 percent.

By then, I was no longer on the edge every day and, as my friends would say, could relax and smell the roses a little. Yet, I found myself at a career crossroads. For me, the fun comes in ripping something apart, figuring out how to fix it, and eventually succeeding in making it better than before. I began to wonder if I had used up my bag of tricks at Stephens and whether it might be time for someone else, with a new perspective, to lead the college.

Still, I wasn't looking for a new opportunity when an acquaintance recommended me to the search committee at Stetson University. Florida didn't exactly intrigue me, but I agreed to the interview out of respect for my friend. Well, I quickly discovered that central Florida is fabulous. Second, I could see that Stetson and I were a good fit; the strategic planning experience and financial skills I had developed as a business officer matched much of what the university needed. In 2009, I became Stetson's ninth president (and the first woman to hold the position).

A Sporting Chance

At our historic main campus in DeLand, Florida, Stetson University has the College of Arts and Sciences, School of Business Administration, and School of Music. We also have a satellite campus near Orlando, plus the College of Law located 150 miles away, near St. Petersburg—and the law school has a satellite campus in Tampa. One of the interesting challenges—not only for the CFO but also the entire leadership—is how to become a more unified university without forcing everyone to do everything in the same way. I see Stetson as one 501(c)(3), with one budget and one university administration. Still, we have to allow our units to flower on their own because of their strengths, rather than straitjacket them into things that may not work well.

On the historic campus, we've undertaken infrastructure improvements, such as major landscaping projects, carbon-footprint reduction, and classroom renovations; these are part of a new campus master plan to guide future growth.

We developed constellations of academic excellence to highlight and invest in our academic strengths. To better recruit and retain students, we've enhanced residential life by purchasing an apartment complex for student housing and offering pet-friendly residence halls. And, we have dramatically expanded athletics by introducing a club sports program and adding Division I women's lacrosse and sand volleyball.

The most noticeable change in athletics, however, will occur in the fall of 2013 when football returns to Stetson University after a 57-year absence. More than 100 men have already signed declarations of intent to play for the new team, and we were fortunate to hire a coach who understands that Stetson wants scholars first and football players second. That's simply the way it has to be because of who Stetson is. In fact, we expect players on all our teams, no matter what the sport, to be scholars first. Athletics is part of a young person's full development at Stetson but not the only focus.

Of course, expanding into football at a time when resources are already tight—and when some faculty may believe athletic programs already command too much of the university's money—may look like the wrong way to go. And, I would agree, if Stetson were building a football program based on athletic scholarships. We are joining the Pioneer Football League, which—like the Ivy League—does not allow athletic scholarships.

Football makes significantly more sense when viewed as part of the strategic plan, as one means of attracting students from different geographies who come in at about the same discount rate as other students. For Stetson, football is about enrollment, more men on campus, and campus vibrancy on the weekends.

Pricing and Delivery

At a recent meeting of college presidents, the talk turned to the intersection of learning, value, and cost. In other words, how do you deliver the kind of learning that young people and their families expect from your institution? And, how do you provide the value they expect at a price they can afford?

Between the natural pressures on private higher education and the state financing pressures within public higher education, every institution has made substantial cuts. We are not an industry of fluff anymore—if we ever were. Yet, the marketplace remains very confused about the cost of higher education. In the private sector, in particular, people seem to think there's still an awful lot we can cut. They don't understand how much of every tuition dollar goes back to families. A substantial amount of gift and endowment revenue supports every student as well—without tax subsidies.

Families like to send their children to us because higher education develops the whole person. That's why, in addition to academics, you need athletics, student services, counseling, and rock-climbing walls—or whatever the must-have feature is this year. But, those programs and services all have costs. And, those programs and services don't necessarily make the education we deliver any better—they just make the wrapping paper prettier.

Within higher education, we're engaged in an interesting "arms race" with one another. If one institution adds or does something, others feel compelled to match the action or up the ante. In my mind, I keep wondering which brave institutions will step forward and say, "Enough! We must stop using this pricing model and start pricing education right where we need to." We need enough schools with enough market clout to change the pricing structure—but I don't see that happening anytime soon.

One of my colleagues, a college president, has remarked that faculty will eventually become coaches and mentors, leaving technology to deliver the content. In a residential environment like Stetson's, I have trouble imagining that the role of the faculty would wither to that extent. But, we need to be openly pushing the frontier of how technology can deliver not a cheaper education but a better one.

The questions around technology remind me of discussions about assessment. We do some valuable things that are not quantifiable. You simply can't measure everything that's important to the educational experience. Similarly, you can employ technology to improve education—but just becoming a technologically sophisticated university doesn't mean you are delivering an excellent learning experience. Any tool has to be tied to student learning and why the institution exists.

So, no need for me to be bored in today's environment. Lots to noodle on and improve for the sake of all who love our institutions or will come to do so.

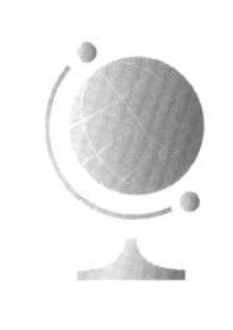

THE INTERNATIONAL VIEW

By Joseph P. Mullinix

JOSEPH P. MULLINIX

Joseph "Joe" P. Mullinix serves as deputy president (administration) for the National University of Singapore. Before moving abroad in 2006, he spent six years as senior vice president for business and finance at the University of California system and seven years as vice president for finance and administration at Yale University. He also worked at Columbia University for nearly a decade, ultimately serving as CBO.

Mullinix has a BA in economics from Georgetown University, earned his MBA from the University of Chicago, and pursued graduate studies at Harvard Business School. Outside of higher education, his experience includes working at Goldman Sachs as a senior financial analyst; at Arthur Young as an auditor; and in the Office of Management and Budget as deputy associate director, economics and government. In addition to serving as chair of the NACUBO Board of Directors, Mullinix has been a board member of several higher education associations and of numerous nonprofits focused on neighborhood development, social service delivery, health care, and the arts.

THE INTERNATIONAL VIEW

My father had very little education, but he and my mother placed a high priority on academic achievement. Good grades—the product of lots of parental encouragement—gained me an opportunity to attend a competitive high school, where my notable lack of athletic prowess and artistic talent steered me toward debate as my extracurricular activity of choice. A love of numbers and debate led me to Georgetown University for an undergraduate degree in economics and the University of Chicago business school for my MBA. I am incredibly grateful for these educational experiences and the scholarships that made them possible.

My first real job was in New York City as an Arthur Young auditor and consultant. Then, the U.S. military called for two years on active duty as an Army officer. Upon returning to civilian life, a Chrysler Fellowship led to study at the Harvard Business School. Three years later, writing a dissertation on health care and planning an academic career with my biochemist wife, I faced the harsh realities of reduced science funding, two-career job hunting, and another small mouth to feed. Our dreams of a career in academia seemed to vanish.

A move to Washington, D.C., enabled us to find good jobs in the same city. My wife was a National Institutes of Health researcher, and I joined the U.S. Office of Management and Budget (OMB), ultimately becoming deputy associate director for economics and government. A decade later, we returned to New York, where my wife joined Columbia as a vice provost, and I joined Goldman Sachs as a senior financial analyst.

From Interim to Permanent

At Goldman, I enjoyed the work and learned a lot from my colleagues—who were incredibly smart and principled. However, I missed the social purpose that had guided work at the federal government and much of the consulting. The job at Goldman was pretty demanding on a two-career family that now had three young children. In 1984, thinking (probably not too clearly) that higher education would place fewer demands on my time and get me back to beloved academia, I joined the staff at Columbia University in New York.

The interim position, as a vice provost, involved establishing a more analytical framework for strengthening academic and financial planning. It was a big transition from the federal executive offices and investment banking to academia. I wasn't an immediate success at Columbia. I recall, with amusement now, a meeting early in my tenure at which I proposed what I mistakenly thought was a modest change in the budgeting process. The Arts and Sciences vice president turned "beet red" as he announced that some new guy in the provost's office was not going to put his funds at risk. I slowly learned new sensitivities and, ultimately, earned acceptance by helping to expand student housing, restore a decaying physical plant, and introduce new IT systems. It wasn't my original dream of academia, but I enjoyed the work and the people.

The year or two I expected to stay at Columbia turned into a decade. I became the senior vice president responsible for nonfinancial administrative and student support. Watching a sea of young people mature and trying to assist in that process with new community assistance programs, better counseling, and more student events made those years particularly rewarding. A few years later, I was appointed the CBO, responsible for both financial and administration programs.

In 1993, an opportunity opened up at Yale, where Rick Levin was about to become president. Although I hadn't really thought about continuing my career in higher education, I was excited by his vision for the university and became Yale's vice president for finance and administration. The early '90s were not the best of times at Yale, with budget deficits and substantial deferred maintenance. The challenge of bringing this wonderful campus to its full potential and assisting in getting a fundamentally sound institution back on a road of financial equilibrium was one that could not be resisted.

Heading West

A change in my personal life made an opportunity to head west—to become the senior vice president for business and finance at the University of California (UC) system—seem particularly attractive at the start of the new millennium. Some folks questioned my judgment, as the rapidly expanding system (adding 5,000 additional undergraduates a year) faced many challenges. System positions also don't have many of the intrinsic rewards of a campus and often focus on the "problem du jour."

It took some time to appreciate the differences between public and private institutions. Columbia and Yale had the luxury of defining their societal roles—the types of students they serve, the education they offer, and so forth—and were accountable to a relatively defined group of stakeholders. The people within a state and their business and political leaders drive the mandate of public educational institutions. UC admission was practically an entitlement for qualified California residents; serving this divergent and rapidly growing population was a challenging reality for UC.

Working in a system office offered an amazing opportunity to explore new and diverse areas, from management of multiple national labs and medical centers to the development of a new campus and substantial expansion of existing facilities. The range of experiences was broader than I could have imagined, and the scale of opportunities—as well as challenges—was continually surprising.

From my earliest days at Columbia, I had always been intrigued by the potential for enhancing the classroom experience through the use of technology. The focus of Columbia and Yale on small class size, as well as the conceptual and economic challenges in that environment, seemed to limit this potential. With a big system, expanding enrollments, and many large sections, UC seemed an opportune environment for such investments in technology innovation in the classroom. Campuses wouldn't have to offer the same courses, but together they could develop and share modules and technological innovations to enhance the classroom experience.

Similarly, I naively assumed that the opportunities for sharing or integrating services with other campuses would be much simpler in a system than in the Ivy environment. There were indeed many UC system-wide programs and collaborations between individual campuses, but the challenges to more substantial integration were very similar to my earlier experiences. Each campus valued its autonomy, was at a different stage of development with divergent immediate priorities, and had a natural skepticism about the rewards of common systems. Independent campus development had served the system well. Even when there was agreement on a common strategy, a lack of resources and competing priorities in a difficult period limited progress.

Sharing Problems and Solutions

One aspect of higher education I've always loved is its open, collegial atmosphere. When I worked in Goldman Sachs, for example, it was always a challenge to get advice and information from colleagues in other banks. But, through NACUBO, the regions, and groups like the Ivy League Business Officers, I had the ability to meet other business officers, share problems, and ask for help. Our institutions are often competitors, but we share information to enhance all institutions. As someone who came from outside higher education, I found these groups invaluable in helping me adjust to a new environment as well as providing ideas for solving problems.

Fortunately, the CFOs of the Big 10, plus the University of Chicago and, strangely, the California system—helped me acclimate when I moved from private to public education. In addition, 10 CBOs from the UC campuses provided tutorials on California and public education.

On a personal level, NACUBO, the regional associations, and other higher education professional groups provided me with an opportunity for personal development and great friendships with colleagues and participants from government and industry.

An Ocean Away

Every year in California brought more funding challenges and hot political issues. After six years, I thought about exploring opportunities outside of higher education. Having had three great jobs, at three wonderful institutions, I doubted my ability to find a different but equally compelling college or university position.

Then, a recruiter called about a position in Singapore. Never having seriously considered a job outside the United States, it took me some time to conclude that Asia was probably the most exciting place in higher education today, and Singapore was the perfect spot in Asia for me. In 2006, I moved a little farther west to become deputy president of administration at the National University of Singapore (NUS). This position oversees the business and financial activities of Singapore's largest university.

While U.S. colleges and universities are extraordinary, my NUS experience and impressions suggest that the U.S. educational system should not be complacent. For instance:

- In Singapore, you need to think and act much faster than at most U.S. universities. Singapore, itself, is very entrepreneurial and moves at a fast pace, and that culture carries over to the university.
- Throughout Asia, there's a hunger to do more, to excel, to grow, and to compete. There is not the sense of self-satisfaction that sometimes creeps into U.S. institutions.
- Most Asian countries are spending more, not less, on tertiary education.
- The United States and the United Kingdom are still the places that most Asian universities look for best practices to emulate. But, Japan, Korea, Hong Kong, and Singapore—as well as fast-rising China and India—have supported strong university growth and exhibit an appreciation for education that, to some extent, has faded in the United States, as skepticism about all institutions has grown.
- In Singapore, the K-12 preparation of the students is amazing. Some students fall behind their U.S. counterparts in their English oral and written expressive abilities, but these students are fluent in Mandarin (or one of the two other recognized "mother tongues") and often have learned a dialect that is spoken at home. The students are more focused on getting an education than many U.S. students and typically are strong in science and math.

Innovative approaches to challenges might also be easier for newer and growing universities. For example, NUS has chosen to partner with other institutions rather than launch many new initiatives on its own. NUS believes partnering to obtain expertise gives it a better product, faster and at less expense.

NUS partners with the Peabody Institute of Johns Hopkins for the development and operation of a conservatory for western music, with Duke University for the development and operation of the Duke-NUS Graduate Medical School, and more recently, with Yale University for the development of a new Yale-NUS College with a liberal arts curriculum. NUS doesn't simply copy the American courses and programs and import them as a whole. It works with its partners to incorporate lessons learned by them to enhance their curriculums and teaching methods, and then incorporates new elements to reflect a more international approach to make a program appropriate for Asia in the 21st century.

Similarly, NUS has also developed an enormous array of joint-degree, dual-degree, double-major, and exchange programs with major institutions around the world to complement its offerings. It has launched innovative programs with universities and start-up entities in China, Israel, India, Sweden, and the United States to develop entrepreneurial skills. Similarly, research universities from around the world have complementary ongoing projects at the NUS campus.

Challenges and Rewards

Looking on from afar after three decades in higher education administration, I am continually amazed at the additional burdens on U.S. higher education from legal and regulatory mandates as well as rising expectations from parents, students, and the public. Some regulations undoubtedly provide valued safeguards, and recreational facilities that would make country club managers drool—or dining options that are inconceivable even to most parents—undoubtedly add to the quality of student life. But, one must wonder if most would be happier with a lower term bill in lieu of these enhancements, or perhaps a little more on the margins invested in education. Rising expectations certainly extend beyond U.S. borders, but most foreign universities are far less burdened by such mandates and expectations.

Similarly, all universities face pressures from needs for new research facilities, but the overall impact seems more severe in the United States. These cost pressures have driven up the cost of education at a time when many governments are feeling financial strain and attempting to reduce support to education, returns on investments are no longer robust, and parents and prospective students face less certain financial times.

These expanded pressures have contributed to the expanding role of the CBO—of which there are fewer and fewer these days, probably because it's difficult to find experienced financial leaders who also have expertise in HR, IT, and construction. More CBO jobs are being split into multiple vice presidents reporting to the president, which often leads to a diminution of the business and financial function. I find that trend unfortunate, especially since provosts are taking on more operational responsibilities beyond the traditional chief academic officer function and could benefit from a close partnership with strong business leaders.

My three decades in higher education administration were not part of a career plan, but they have been incredibly rewarding. I have been very fortunate to have worked with supportive colleagues and staff at great institutions and had opportunities to contribute to their growth and improvement, providing more opportunities for students to experience a better quality education.

As a former student who spent nine years in higher education that transformed my life, I find great satisfaction in helping others to have a similar experience. And, I experience continual renewal participating in the process by which students and faculty continually transform the university as they bring new knowledge, methods of learning, and ways of expression that prepare the university for the next generation of students.

FROM STUDENT TO STAFF

By Nim Chinniah

NIM CHINNIAH

Nim Chinniah is vice president for administration and CFO at the University of Chicago, where his responsibilities also include fiscal and strategic planning and supporting four trustee committees. Previously, he spent 16 years at Vanderbilt University in a variety of positions, which culminated in his serving as deputy vice chancellor for administration and academic affairs.

Chinniah earned a BS in computer science and business from Lambuth University in Jackson, Tennessee (now the Lambuth campus of the University of Memphis), and his MBA from Vanderbilt. His recognitions include receiving NACUBO's Rising Star Award and being named a 2011 Business Leader of Color by Chicago United. In 2011, he was also a finalist for the Chicago CFO of the Year Award presented by Financial Executives International. In addition to numerous professional affiliations, Chinniah currently serves on the governing boards of Chicago Children's Choir and University of Chicago Charter Schools.

FROM STUDENT TO STAFF

In 1987, I left Sri Lanka to attend a small liberal arts college in Jackson, Tennessee. In 2011, that Methodist institution where I earned my bachelor's degree closed its doors after 168 years. It had a very small endowment and was almost totally dependent on tuition from about 800 students; the U.S. financial crisis proved the tipping point for a college that had struggled for years.

That story, unfortunately, is not unique. Other small private institutions with troubled financial models may have to follow a similar path as Lambuth University, which now exists as a campus of the University of Memphis. Like banks, telecommunications companies, and hospitals throughout the United States, smaller educational institutions may have to consolidate or be absorbed by larger institutions.

The scarcity of resources means that all institutions, no matter their size, must get better at what they do. Those of us within institutions need to be very thoughtful about setting priorities—and then executing those priorities.

The Right Place

Upon completion of my bachelor's degree in computer science and business, I earned my masters of business administration at Vanderbilt. Through an internship at Vanderbilt between my first and second years, I developed a respect for the scale of operations within higher education. I decided that the breadth of a major research university represented exactly the kind of environment in which I wanted to work.

Having known the university as a student, I was fortunate to gain the experience of seeing Vanderbilt from the other side, as an administrator. In 1991, right out of business school, I held the first of several positions in what became a 16-year career at Vanderbilt. Initially, I worked as an internal consultant in the finance and administrative areas, with a focus on the information systems department. In the early 1990s, for example, we were moving away from mainframes, so I did all the business and financial planning for the transition to an ERP system.

Some assignments can take your professional development down interesting paths. At one point, Vanderbilt offered me the opportunity to manage the president's residence. Most people would have advised, "Don't take the job because the residence is not only the president's home but also a university center, all rolled into one." But, I did take the job, which included managing about 200 special events at the residence each year. In the process, I learned how to work directly with a president and, in particular, got to know Vanderbilt's chancellor, Gordon Gee.

Gordon and Lauren Brisky, the CFO, were thoughtful and intentional about preparing me for the next job, both personally and professionally. They gave me opportunities to work on special projects and a lot of exposure to the board. In my last three years at Vanderbilt, I split my role between supporting the CFO and the provost. As deputy vice chancellor for administration and academic affairs, I served as the CFO for the academic enterprise—the 10 schools that reported to the provost. In addition, I managed all the business administrative operations for the CFO, including the police department, plant operations, real estate, dining, traffic and parking, bookstores, registrar, and the golf course.

Straddling the two areas gave me both a financial and administrative portfolio. It also emphasized to me that, in addition to technical skills, a CBO needs to develop other skills—how to communicate, how to negotiate, how to influence, and how to work with people who don't have a similar background and training. The varied learning opportunities I had at Vanderbilt have served me well, especially now that I am vice president for administration and CFO at the University of Chicago.

Growing Responsibilities

My position has changed in the five years I have been at the University of Chicago. When I first arrived, I focused more on the financial enterprise because we had a new president and a financial plan that needed to catch up with the strategic plan. Now, my role is more on the strategic side, not only financially but also operationally.

In the past, someone in my position would have been viewed as being responsible for a set of activities that needed to get done quietly and mostly behind the scenes. Today, the role requires being a much more visible partner and a senior advisor. In my CFO role, for example, I report to the president but work for and with the provost, the deans, and the head of the medical center. It isn't just a hierarchical relationship; they are my partners. That means I have to work with a variety of people whose roles are very different from mine, while understanding the connectivity between those roles.

When I first came to the University of Chicago in 2007, I needed to establish my credibility with the academic side and prove myself as a partner, as someone who understood its world. I had to demonstrate I was engaged in what was happening in the university—not just somebody who worried about compliance and policy. When my phone started ringing, I knew I had succeeded: Deans started calling with problems and asking for help.

My job is to help solve problems and support their work, not only in the context of our financial envelope but also in the context of what's the responsible and reasonable thing to do. As long as my teams and I can be part of that solution, rather than a hindrance, the deans will keep coming back to us, which helps the entire enterprise. I might delegate—say, ask someone to work with an associate dean on a problem—but I stay close to the issue and watch what happens. If it is important for the dean, it is important for me.

In addition to being a "fixer" of problems, I am a senior advisor to the president—and that is another change from how my position might have been viewed a decade ago. The issues the president and I discuss go far beyond finances. Since I started, the president has broadened my position to include more operational responsibilities. For example, he added the police department and IT to my portfolio, which also includes facilities, HR, risk management and audit, environmental health and safety, financial services, business diversity, and real estate.

The chief information officer used to report directly to the president, and the University of Chicago Police Department's chief used to report to the vice president for civic engagement. The president decided both would report to me instead because everything in my area has operational intensity. Policing, IT operations, utilities, and emergency response all have a 24/7 nature, so it made sense to group them together for greater synergy and efficiency. When an alarm goes off on campus, the situation almost always has a physical facilities component, in addition to a police component in terms of our response. IT underpins all of that, whether by providing access to our buildings or access to footage from security cameras. We can bring people together much more seamlessly with the functions housed in one area.

An Integrated Approach

At the University of Chicago, we talk constantly about the culture of planning and execution. If the president or the provost represents the plan—what we are trying to do—then I represent the execution—how to get it done. To align planning and execution, you have to have all the appropriate people together in the same room. So, I need to be at the table when the planning is done, and the president or provost needs to partner with me in the execution. Our provost and our president both understand our financial picture every bit as well as I do.

It can be a strategic advantage for a university to have respectful engagement of all three roles. When you execute a plan that everybody understands and agrees with, the provost and CFO don't waste time arguing—or trying to outmaneuver each other to convince the president which way to do something.

Once a month, on behalf of the president, I convene and chair a working group that includes the chief investment officer, the CFO for the medical center, and the treasurer. We talk about strategic and operational issues in terms of liquidity, banking relationships, pension funding, and so forth so we can integrate our planning in those areas. We also have the Financial Strategy Group, chaired by the president, which includes the provost, the chief investment officer, the chief development officer, the CFO for the medical center, and me. Twice a month, that group looks at issues of financial impact, such as the financial assumptions that drive our long-range model.

Through these groups, we've created internal transparency. All of us have a clear sense, for example, of the liquidity within our endowment. We understand our debt strategy and our debt profile. Then, we can use that knowledge to inform the fund-raising goals set for the head of development. And, since he's in the room with us, he knows why we need x dollars per year. It's very clear that, without those x dollars, we can't meet the needs of our strategic plan. By taking such an intentional approach to integrating planning and execution, we don't have people being surprised by or second-guessing decisions.

I occasionally take thoughts from these meetings and raise them with the chair of one of the four board committees I staff. I might say, "Here is how we are thinking about a particular issue. Have we missed anything? From your vantage point, what else might we want to consider?" These committees include credible leaders within the business community, so I like to engage them as members of our extended team; I'm also fortunate that our trustees respect the boundary between board and management. We are able to use their expertise and commitment to the institution in the most appropriate areas, and they appreciate the opportunity to be more engaged with the university.

Future Focus

Looking ahead, I see several challenges for higher education, particularly large research institutions. First, public pressure for increased accountability for research dollars will continue to rise, continuing a trend that started about five years ago. People want to know how they benefit from giving institutions $400 or $500 million a year in research funding.

With this greater focus on the impact of research will come the need to better communicate both the benefits of research activities and the value they add to society. Universities tend to be very quiet about everything we do, and that needs to change. We need to become much more effective in talking about what we really do—especially to elected officials—by sharing our successes and communicating how our research helps the community at large.

If the predictions come true and research funding changes, or the growth rate flattens, we will see even greater collaboration across disciplines and across universities. And, that leads to another challenge: recruiting and retaining the very best faculty. I don't think research funding is given to institutions; it's given to the people in those institutions. In other words, research funding follows faculty.

So, if you do not invest in the facilities and programs that will keep the faculty at your institution, you will see your research funding follow the faculty right out the door.

At the same time, if universities in other countries start retaining their talent, U.S. institutions will be greatly impacted. At the University of Chicago, for example, a third of our faculty are non-U.S. citizens. A powerful piece of our human capital comes from other parts of the world, which are now building great facilities and attempting to duplicate what the United States has done in higher education.

Where will our human capital come from in the next 10 to 15 years? Already, I'm seeing more students from other countries return home after earning their degrees in the United States, which is different from my generation of immigrants. And, as opportunities expand elsewhere, some students may not come to the United States at all for their education. My sister in Sri Lanka, for example, has two teenage sons, and neither seems to feel the same pressure I did to leave the country and go to the United States. Things have changed much in just a 25-year span.

When I think about the CFO job now—and in the future—two words come to mind. One is *stewardship*: We are entrusted with these great universities, and our job is to leave them better than we found them.

The other word is *legacy*: We really have to think about how the decisions made today will impact the next generation of leadership. In many respects, we will be judged by the next generation, and the generation after that, in terms of what we have done and how effective those accomplishments have been.

I have definitely thought about what I would like the person sitting in my position 20 or 30 years from now to say about my contribution to the University of Chicago. I'd like to be remembered as someone who made sustainable change and contributed to a culture of excellence that marries planning and execution. I'd like to think my stewardship positioned the university to not only dream big but also consistently deliver on what it sets out to do. I would hope my legacy is that I contributed to making a great university even better.

AN EXPANDING PORTFOLIO

By Patricia A. Charlton

PATRICIA A. CHARLTON

Patricia "Patty" A. Charlton joined the College of Southern Nevada (formerly Community College of Southern Nevada) in 1995. As senior vice president and chief of the president's staff, she oversees finance, facilities, technology management, HR, the police department, emergency management and preparedness, and several other areas. Her previous experience includes working in the Department of Energy, where she handled budget development and contract negotiations.

In addition to serving on several committees of the Nevada System of Higher Education, Charlton is a member of site visitation teams for the Northwest Association of Colleges and Universities. A former board member of NACUBO and WACUBO, Charlton graduated from the Community College of Southern Nevada with an associate's degree in business management. She also holds a BS in business administration and an MPA, both from the University of Nevada, Las Vegas.

AN EXPANDING PORTFOLIO

In the wake of the terrorist attacks of September 11, 2001, the U.S. hotel industry saw room occupancies plummet as wary tourists and business travelers chose destinations closer to home. Las Vegas felt the brunt of this stagnation, and our shrinking hotel industry laid off thousands of employees. And, in the aftermath, where did the newly unemployed turn for retraining? They turned to us—the College of Southern Nevada (CSN), the community college in Las Vegas.

At CSN, we're accustomed to having companies, public safety groups, and casinos come to us seeking customized programs or training activities for their employees. Typically, we can design a program within a short period of time—that's how responsive our community college faculty can be. To target the needs of former hotel workers seeking new skill sets, we assigned entire sites and campus facilities to offer credit and noncredit programs not previously a part of our curriculum, related to health care and allied health program development. With funding support from the state and other partners, we trained hundreds of people to new competencies, enabling them to gain employment in growing markets, such as health-care services, to serve an aging population.

Back Home Again

When I enrolled at CSN as an 18-year-old student, I didn't know what I wanted to do. I was blessed with great professors and faculty in the accounting and business departments who energized and inspired me. When I graduated, I never imagined returning to work at the same institution that stimulated my career.

Looking back, I realize that joining the staff at CSN was like coming home. CSN, then known as the Community College of Southern Nevada, was located right around the corner from where my childhood home was—I walked to campus for my classes and earned my associate's degree in business management. I later added a bachelor's degree (business administration) and a master's degree (public administration) from the University of Nevada, Las Vegas to my educational arsenal.

Early in my career, I discovered that a unique aspect of the community college environment is that business and industry turn to community colleges to supply trained workers. Over the years, Nevada has been dependent upon a limited number of industries—predominantly gaming, defense, and mining. When one or more of those segments falls into decline, the negative effects send a wave throughout the state's economic base.

I felt those ripples in the early 1990s after working for a contractor to the Department of Energy whose primary role was to support underground testing. I worked specifically for the general manager's office and office of legal affairs. After the Berlin Wall came down and the Cold War ended, the whole world changed—and so did Nevada's economic environment, as defense-related work evaporated and the weapons testing program was discontinued.

In 1995, I applied for an opening at CSN that perfectly fit my skill set. My business office "toolbox" and skills were portable and transferred easily from government to higher education. In fact, when I interviewed for the job at the college, the search committee included one of my former teachers! When the CBO position opened up at CSN, some of my greatest sources of encouragement to pursue my dream were our faculty—the same faculty who encouraged an 18-year-old to explore the field of finance and accounting. My work at CSN is more than a job—it is an opportunity for me to give back to the people who have been so supportive of me and my aspirations throughout my career.

Today, as CSN's senior vice president of finance and administration and chief of the president's staff, I think I have the best job on campus. Through my work with our associated students, I'm here to help the students meet their goals. I get to work with all our employee groups and reassure them that our financial ship is stable so that they can concentrate on doing the best job they can. And, I work with the faculty—the group of people who were instrumental in shaping my own life direction.

Multiple Roles

Repercussions from the U.S. economic downturn have had a sustained impact on Nevada's economy; every year since 2005, the state has cut CSN's budget. Nevada is not out of the financial woods yet. As a result, our main focus is to make sure we are smart, efficient, and accountable for how we use the resources we do have.

For instance, we have developed internal committees comprised of faculty, staff, and students that have assisted our efforts in making cost reductions. Because many faculty and managers within higher education don't come from a business model, I try to offer recommendations for streamlining functions or operations. Our president is committed to providing transparency regarding our financial situation and strives to be inclusive in decision making that will affect us institutionally. Although senior administration will ultimately make the tough decisions on what will be reduced or cut, we want and need to hear all the voices of the people who will be impacted by those changes.

My inclusion on that leadership team is one sign of how the business officer role has evolved. Historically, business officers sat in the back room and were tasked to ensure the lights were on, the budgets were solid, and all those pesky little reports were completed. Now, we are more at the forefront, working alongside presidents and provosts. Our visibility has greatly increased, both on and off campus, and to internal and external constituents.

In some respects, my role changes from day to day. I might be a psychologist one day, talking with employees concerned about their jobs and worrying about whether we can afford to retain them. The next day I might be the public information officer, getting involved in discussions with the media, legislators, the foundation, trustees, and business and industry representatives.

These external audiences want to hear straight talk about how sustainable our business model is. The old model—where we increased our fees and budgets every year—is gone. In Nevada, we are moving toward a new funding model that would include performance-based measures established by legislators or other external groups. We look forward to implementing performance metrics—this will provide another opportunity to be transparent to our communities and stakeholders.

My job includes communicating a community college's differences from a university or a comprehensive doctoral institution. People don't always come to us for a degree. Sometimes they simply want to sharpen their skills or develop new competencies to get in line for that better-paying job, or to prepare for transfer to a four-year school. To us, those students who accomplished what they intended to when they came to CSN are successes, although the rest of the world may see it a little differently. Given the external pressures to increase the percentage of graduates, I anticipate some tough years ahead as higher education works out the appropriate metrics.

Behind the move toward metrics is the bigger issue of accountability. Not only do we have greater regulatory compliance than in years past, but also we have to battle increased questions from the general public. As tuition and registration rates have risen significantly, the people who support our institutions want to know, quite rightly, that we are using their money in the most effective ways possible.

Our donors want to know how we'll use their dollars—how we will manage and make the most of the resources they give us. The business office has always supported fund-raising initiatives, but now I'm much more involved with our development office on the ground-floor efforts.

The Next 50

In just the last three years, my position has expanded in ways that I could never have anticipated. CSN has a total of three vice presidents, including me. Whatever doesn't fall into academic affairs or student affairs now reports to me, including technology, police, HR, and auxiliary services. I'm constantly learning about new areas that are critically important to our institution, such as emergency management and preparedness.

In addition to my role as the CFO of CSN, I'm also the president's chief of staff, the person with whom the president consults on a wide range of issues. In this role, I coordinate various efforts and activities with the other vice presidents, who see me as an advisor on various issues and initiatives. And, when the president is not here, I take on his leadership role.

Another significant change has been my evolving relationship with the academic side of the house. I spend more time with the academic vice president than ever before—which makes sense, because academics are where we utilize most of our resources and represent the "core" of our business. We bounce a lot of ideas and "What ifs?" off one another to ensure that we're moving in the right direction, not just for the current year but also for the future.

Fifty years from now, it's difficult to say what my business officer successor might be doing because higher education will change exponentially in the next 25 years and will continue to evolve in the years after. Within the next 10 years alone, most publicly funded institutions will become publicly *aided*—in other words, our primary source of money will no longer come from state or local sources.

Here are some developments I foresee happening within higher education:

In general, higher education will become leaner. I wouldn't be surprised to see more institutions melding together the vice presidential roles of student affairs and academic affairs. That would mean the CBO will continue to inherit anything that doesn't fit on the academic/student sides of the house.

Even though CBOs will divert time and attention from strictly fiscal matters, they will still need strong financial knowledge and expertise. Financial reporting and accountability will, however, remain the most visible part of their expanding portfolio. I have worked for 10 presidents, who all agreed on this. Business officers need to have a strong grasp of finance and operations and will always be welcomed to the boardroom, at the state capitol, or anywhere on campus.

Many business officers will follow the path to a college or university presidency. Historically, presidents have come from the academic side of the house, but the public is more frequently viewing higher education as a business, desiring leaders with a bottom-line mindset. Internally, with budgets changing along with fluctuating enrollments and funding, a president with a strong financial background who understands the day-to-day flow is advantageous. Some items to look for in the future:

1. In 10 to 20 years, we'll have fewer educational institutions than we do today. Out of pure necessity, the remaining colleges and universities will be smaller and leaner. Our constituencies will demand that we embrace reform, increase transparency, and show greater accountability for our use of the resources they provide.
2. The traditional semester model, where you need 16 weeks to take an English or science class, will change. Community colleges already offer short-term

classes, which are expected to grow in popularity as the traditional student population decreases and more students want to move in and out of higher education at a speedier pace.

3. Especially in the public arena, business officers will need to become more skilled at navigating external politics. We will have to work closely with legislators and government officials who live a world away from higher education.

4. Communication skills will be critically important for business officers. We need to use our financial knowledge to explain and persuade our users and partners of the challenges, successes, and contributions that community colleges, universities, and doctoral institutions can offer to our cities, states, and nation. We must address the "language barrier" that precludes us from reaching all of our college community—our donors, legislators, and all others who have a vested interest in our success.

One thing won't change for business officers—the need to have a good balance in their lives. These jobs pull you in many different directions at any given time. You have to take the time to stop, look in the mirror, and assess and feel good about the decisions you have made. Your family will keep you grounded—and so will holding tightly to your core principles and values.

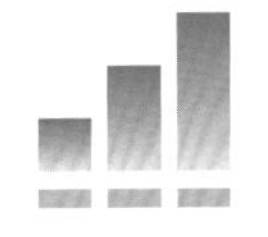

BUILDING ON THE BEST OF THE PAST

By James E. Morley, Jr.

JAMES E. MORLEY, JR.

James "Jay" E. Morley, Jr., past president and CEO of NACUBO, lives in Annapolis, Maryland, and consults with colleges and universities on matters related to governance, financial, administrative, and organizational management. Before joining NACUBO in 1995, he served as senior vice president at Cornell University and held senior financial and administrative roles at three other universities.

Prior to his experience in higher education, Morley worked at Ernst & Ernst and served five years in the U.S. Marine Corps; he is a retired colonel, USMC Reserve. The coauthor of *The Extraordinary Higher Education Leader* (2001), Morley has received NACUBO's Distinguished Business Officer award and serves on the governing boards of several educational institutions. He holds a BS in mechanical engineering from Rensselaer Polytechnic Institute and an MS in accounting from Syracuse University.

BUILDING ON THE BEST OF THE PAST

Over the past 50 years, the college and university world has felt the effects of increasing government oversight, skyrocketing energy costs, changing student demographics and enrollment, and decreasing levels of government funding. Every disruption was greeted with, "This will pass." It appears, however, that the challenges from 21st-century economic and market forces will remain persistent and unforgiving. Going forward, things will surely be different—and the solutions that worked in the past will not suffice for the future.

A strikingly different future notwithstanding, several bedrock principles have created and sustained the U.S. network of public and private colleges and universities that remains the envy of the world. These basic values and principles include the following:

- Academic freedom
- Shared governance
- Institutional governing autonomy
- Decentralized decision making
- Access for all
- Education as a public good

These fundamental aspects have served nonprofit and public colleges and universities well. The future must be shaped by using the best of what the past has to offer as the base for building a vibrant, new future for traditional colleges and universities. As a member of an institution's senior leadership team, the CBO must join in studying these essential values and principles and applying them within the context of today's challenges and opportunities.

An Evolving Role

Here's a rough approximation of how the historical financial model in higher education worked: Trustees (at a private institution), state legislatures (for a public institution), and central administration built the institution, its academic program, and student services; students enrolled; faculty taught; students graduated; and alumni gave money back to their alma mater. The traditional role of the CBO was as the institution's "chief bookkeeper."

This relic of history began to disappear as presidents and trustees saw the need for more sophisticated financial, business, and administrative management. Finance and administrative staffs grew rapidly to account for and to manage debt, endowments, student aid, and sponsored research. Accountability for decisions, whether small or large, became circumscribed by federal, state, and local laws and regulations because government aid supported enrollment growth.

We are at the dawn of a different world for postsecondary education. Far more than bookkeeping, the daily work of the financial, business, and administrative offices and functions predominantly comprises policy compliance, transaction process management, and related supporting information systems. Through their personal stories, other authors in this book trace this evolving role and point to an irrefutable fact: The skills and knowledge required of the CBO historically will remain relevant and essential for personal and institutional success in the future.

CBOs of the Future

Edmund Burke, the 18th-century British politician, famously observed, "You can never plan the future by the past." Baseball great Yogi Berra put his characteristically unique spin on a similar thought when he said, "The future ain't what it used to be."

In fact, the future state of traditional higher education in the United States will not be the same as the past. Evidence of a different future for the higher education landscape comes with the closings or sales of small private colleges, reduced or frozen compensation for staff, tuition discounts above 50 percent, a growing backlog of deferred maintenance, and so on. While public colleges and universities aren't likely to close, the prognosis is for lower levels of government funding.

So, what do such changes in higher education mean for the person in the CBO position? The bottom line is that the effective CBO of the future must have the skills and personal characteristics to lead the finance and administrative functions as well as be a key contributor of the president's senior team at both the strategic and operational levels.

Specifically, the well-qualified CBO of the future will need to do the following:

- Be a "student" of the emerging economic, financial, and government-regulated institution and cognizant of the idiosyncratic of different institutions
- Possess fundamental personal characteristics, such as ethics, integrity, courage to tell the truth and recommend difficult decisions, perseverance, physical stamina, and an ability to convey essential information and messages
- Exhibit effective leadership and supervisory qualities
- Know his or her personal strengths and weaknesses and be on a constant quest for self-awareness and renewal

Leading the Way

As a leading member of the cabinet, who supports the president and actively engages with the board's senior leadership, the CBO of the future must fulfill four primary duties.

1. **A creative visionary.** Successful outcomes stem from understanding institutional requirements and opportunities—especially how they are shaped by market forces and the economics of the educational industry—and establishing goals and objectives for actions and processes. It will not be the power of the CBO position that gets results, but rather the CBO's compelling logic and communication of relevant information in setting the course of the institution.

New expectations require new skills. Changing institutional requirements will require CBOs to create new organizational, financial, and legal structures—such as collaborative, service-support, sharing programs with local communities and/or other institutions—to provide risk management and asset protection. For example, international and satellite programs require different operational models than the traditional, single-institution model. At the same time, the CBO must continue to perform the basic financial and business objectives that support new and complex academic programs, student services, and administrative functions.

2. **A participative team player.** In addition to being an active and senior member of the president's cabinet, standing committees (such as budget, IT, and governance), and ad hoc task forces, the CBO will have to lead committees charged with effective problem solving; the implementation of new, high-value initiatives; or continuous process improvements.

Delegation and working in teams with various department heads may offer the most challenge to CBOs, who may not be comfortable with the notion of assigning tasks and authority to empowered groups. Yet, committees, when effectively designed, empowered, and led, can become efficient and effective vehicles for achieving lasting solutions across many constituents while balancing controls, risk, and costs.

3. **A strategic partner.** The CBO of today and tomorrow must possess and apply strategies for establishing new and revised policies and procedures as well as aligning the staff and information systems to support such strategies. Policies and processes that worked in the past should be reviewed to determine what might still work and what revisions are warranted.

The CBO of the future will be building new business structures, multinational campuses, and partnerships among higher education institutions—both private and public ones—and for-profit businesses. Responding to these challenges will require the following:

- A general intellectual framework of project and goal analysis
- Problem-solving and analytical skills to participate in senior-level discussions, decisions, and operational performance reviews
- The ability to explain likely institutional consequences of alternative goals and policies
- Knowledge of appropriate legal, financial, and organizational structures to align financial, human, information, and physical resources
- Analytical, political, and communication skills to implement and monitor outcomes and make necessary adjustments
- A level of engagement that ensures continuous improvement in both the administrative and academic functions

4. A key collaborator. As a "cultural traveler" to the academic side, the CBO gains a true understanding of, and appreciation for, teaching, research, public service, academic advising, and student mentoring. This better enables the CBO to work with the president, chief academic officer, and other senior administrators. To plan, design, and implement the financial and administration policies, processes, and systems necessary for future success, the CBO must understand academic needs, motivations, and culture. The best way to reach that understanding is to venture into the heart of the enterprise—into the world of the teacher and the researcher.

Finally, the successful CBO of the future will need to understand and convey the perspective that a college or university is like other business enterprises, subject to the pressures and consequences of a highly competitive marketplace. At the same time, traditional institutions' values, public service, and commitment to the open exchange of knowledge must be preserved in the best interest of our nation and our democratic form of government. This imperative can be accomplished only with a CBO who brings to the president's cabinet exceptional skills in finance and administration as well as a broad range of personal leadership attributes.

We would like to offer a special thank you to Michael Townsley for his contributions in developing this chapter for NACUBO. We recognize his leadership and vision in bringing about a collection of articles covering key topics and issues that will resonate with NACUBO members for years to come.

AFTERWORD

While the biographical articles on the pages you've just read offer a fascinating glimpse into our profession's past, they represent more than a walk down memory lane. In keeping with the theme of NACUBO's 50th anniversary year—"Looking Back, Leading Forward"—the thought leaders featured showed us not only their diverse professional paths and histories but also their perspectives on the future. It was fascinating to learn how many different ways all the contributors prepared for and acquired their leadership positions and also how higher education has changed over the years and where it might be headed.

It's still hard for me to imagine sitting in Mary Lai's shoes and preparing faculty paychecks on a manual typewriter and paying other university employees in cash, with the bills carefully counted out into envelopes. Or facing the tensions introduced onto a campus in the wake of Title IX's enactment that Ben Quillian mentioned. Although at two completely different institution types, Nim Chinniah and his discussion on engaging the president and provost and sharing successes with the community at large coincided directly with Patty Charlton and her view that CBOs need to hone their communication skills and become more skilled at navigating external politics. Joe Mullinix said it best when describing the collegial atmosphere in the CBO profession—where anyone can pick up the phone and ask for help, share problems, and meet other CBOs around the country. In Wendy Libby's case, her network and ability to communicate financial knowledge to stakeholders helped advance her career from CBO to president.

I was amazed to find that even with the rich variety of perspectives, several commonalities appeared:

- The paradigm shift of how the CBO role has expanded to encompass not just "bookkeeping" but legal issues, facilities management to HR, risk assessment, and more.
- The ability to serve as collaborators.
- The necessity of developing strong communication skills for both internal and external audiences.

Because there are so many unanswered questions with the global economic situation and an expanding international focus, higher education is truly on the brink of a radical transformation. With that change, I have no doubt that NACUBO's next 50 years will serve as a valuable resource–housing the knowledge of the business office community in ways we could never have anticipated.

John D. Walda
President & CEO
NACUBO